Text by **Gilbert Summers**

A Distant View of the Castle Rock

In the time of the Romans, the site that was to become Edinburgh would still have been comparatively unmarked by man's activities. Ignoring the defensive possibilities of that dramatic volcanic crag now known as Castle Rock, the legions, beleaguered in the hostile climate of this northern outpost, built the Antonine Wall in turf, underpinned by stone. It stretched across Scotland and ended on the shores of the Forth some miles upstream from Cramond, within the present-day city of Edinburgh. Traces of a Roman fort and a bath-house have been discovered here. But the Romans, under pressure from elsewhere in their European Empire, withdrew their manpower, leaving the northern tribes, collectively known as Picts, to squabble among themselves. It seems likely that the Castle Rock was, by the fifth century, occupied by the Picts, then the Saxons, in a Dark Ages struggle during which time Edinburgh gained its name.

Though named Dun Edin (the fort on the hillside) before the appearance of the Northumbrian King Edwin, this Saxon ruler fortified the Castle Rock in the seventh century. But the northern Picts then pushed their territories southwards as far as the Tweed – and Edwin's Burgh was fixed firmly within what was to become Scotland.

However, Saxon influence in the Lothians remained strong. The centre of the emerging nation of Scotland, which gained its name from the Scots who had meanwhile invaded from Ireland, was originally further north at Scone and Dunfermline. But this changed, following a storm in the Firth of Forth that shipwrecked refugees from the aftermath of the Norman Conquest, far to the south. One of these refugees was Margaret, sister of Edgar Atheling, heir to the 'English' or Saxon throne, but deposed by the events of 1066. Margaret was brought to the court of Scottish King Malcolm III at Dunfermline. They were soon married. Her comparatively

... nus, this saintly Saxon princess emerges from the warring early tribal legends as an important element in the founding of Edinburgh. The oldest building in the city is her chapel, still standing on the Castle Rock 900 years later. Her husband Malcolm died in battle at Alnwick in Northumberland in 1093 and Margaret outlived him by a few days only. At this time, a little township would have already been spilling down the eastern slopes, clinging to this place of gorse and harsh grasses on either side of a single main street, which was to become the top end of the Royal Mile of today. By the twelfth century, Edinburgh was a walled town, with its eastern boundary somewhere near the Tron Kirk in the High Street.

Malgré son potentiel stratégique, le site d'Edimbourg fut dans l'ensemble ignoré des Romains. Ceux-ci bâtirent le mur D'Antoine en travers du pays, puis, sollicités dans d'autres parties de l'empire, cédèrent la place aux tribus pictes. Ces dernières auraient occupé Castle Rock au 5e siècle, suivies par les Saxons.

C'est d'ailleurs un roi saxon, Edwin, qui donna son nom à la cité (Edwin's Burgh devenant Edinburgh) lorsqu'il fortifia Castle Rock au 7e siècle. Edimbourg devint le centre de la nation naissante (le nom Scotland provenant de la tribu celte des Scots, venus d'Irlande) lorsque Margaret, sœur du prétendant saxon détrôné par Guillaume le Conquérant en 1066, et mariée au roi d'Ecosse Malcolm III, commanda une résidence royale sur Castle Rock.

Sa chapelle, encore debout 900 ans plus tard, est l'édifice le plus ancien de la ville qui, du temps de Margaret (décédée ainsi que son mari en 1093) consistait en une seule rue, ancêtre du présent Royal Mile. Un siècle plus tard, Edimbourg était déjà une ville fortifiée.

Zu römischen Zeiten war das Gelände für das künftige Edinburgh noch völlig unberührt. Die Römer verkannten den strategis-

...eses Felsens und ...e und Steinen den ...Er erstreckte sich ...ottland und endete ...orth of Cramond, ..., das im heutigen ...urgh liegt. Die Römer zogen sich bald zurück und überließen die einheimischen Stämme, die Pikten, ihren Streitigkeiten. Im 5. Jh. wurde der Burgfels wahrscheinlich von den Pikten und dann den Sachsen eingenommen. Aus dieser Ziet rührt auch Edinburgh Name her. Dun Edin (Hügelfeste) hieß es schon, als der sächsische König Edwin von Northumbrien den Burgfelsen im 7. Jh. befestigte. Doch die nördlichen Pikten eroberten diesen Teil zurück und Edwins Burg wurde Teil Schottland.

Der sächsische Einfluß blieb in dieser Gegend erhalten durch die sächsische Prinzessin Margret, Schwester Edgar des Edlen, die den schottischen König Malcolm III. heiratete. Zweifellos war es ihr Einfluß, der zur Erbauung einer königlichen Residenz auf dem Burgfels führte. Das älteste Gebäude der Stadt ist ihre Kapelle, die heute nach 900 Jahren noch immer auf dem Burgfeslen steht. Die Anfänge einer Stadt waren zu dieser Zeit schon sichtbar. Im 12. Jh. war Edinburgh von einer Stadtmauer umgeben und die östliche Grenze war nahe Tron Kirk in der High Street.

Opposite: The Canongate Tolbooth in the mid-nineteenth century. *Front cover: Old Edinburgh* by Patrick and Alexander Nasmyth, 1822. Reproduced by courtesy of the Bank of Scotland, Edinburgh. *Back cover: Cardinal Beaton's House, Cowgate* by Mrs J. Stewart Smith, 1867. By courtesy of Edinburgh City Libraries

Ci-contre: « Canongate Tolbooth » au milieu du dix-neuvième siècle. *En couverture: Le vieil Edimbourg*, de Patrick et Alexander Nasmyth, 1822. *Au dos: La maison du Cardinal Beaton,* « *Cowgate* », de Mme J. Stewart Smith, 1867

Gegenüber: Canongate Tolbooth Mitte des 19. Jhs. *Titelbild: Altes Edinburgh* von Patrick und Alexander Nasmyth, 1822. *Rückseite: Kardinal Beatons Haus, Cowgate* von Mrs. J. Stewart Smith, 1867

Eastward from the Battlements...

Each medieval citizen had his own patch of land, off this embryonic High Street. Wood-framed, turf-thatched cottages stood gable-end on to the main thoroughfare. The soldier on the battlements of Edinburgh Castle would have looked through the haze of wood-smoke to the slopes of Arthur's Seat, still forested in places. Below the wild crags, home of great-antlered deer and wild boar, the Abbey of Holyrood was founded during the reign of David, Margaret's youngest son. Tradition tells of the king's fondness for the hunt. On a day of prayer, he took to horse with his attendants. In a wild pursuit of a stag, he was knocked from his mount by the maddened deer and only saved from further injury by the providential intervention of, either, heavenly voices urging him to found a house of canons, or, the appearance of a cross within the animal's antlers. Some versions of the tale relate that the animal disappeared altogether, leaving the helpless king clutching only the cross. Whatever the truth of the romance, out of gratitude or otherwise, David I granted the Abbey of Holyrood to the Augustinian canons about 1128.

Thus, the link between castle on the crag and abbey – or, eventually, palace – at the lowest end of the downward-sloping mile-long ridge was completed. Meanwhile, the thoroughfare, known as the Royal Mile, between castle and abbey, continued to gain in importance as the spine from which the bones of the old city hung. Its eastern portion, nearest the abbey and below the intersection of Jeffrey and St Mary's Streets with the High Street, is to this day called the Canongate and was once an independent burgh.

Above: Edinburgh Castle by Alexander Nasmyth. Reproduced by courtesy of the National Galleries of Scotland, Edinburgh. *Left:* The Abbey of Holyrood

Ci-dessus: Le château d'Edimbourg, d'Alexander Nasmyth. *A gauche:* L'Abbaye de Holyrood

Oben: Das Edinburgher Schloß von Alexander Nasmyth. *Links:* Die Abtei von Holyrood

Au moyen-âge, chaque habitant d'Edimbourg possédait son lopin de terre situé de part et d'autre de l'embryon de la High Street. C'est au cours du règne de David, fils cadet de Margaret que fut fondée l'abbaye d'Holyrood, vers 1128, à la suite d'un accident de chasse au cours duquel, selon la légende, le roi aurait été sauvé d'une mort certaine par des voix lui ordonnant de fonder une institution religieuse.

Ainsi le lien entre le château au sommet du promontoire et l'abbaye — et plus tard le palais — d'Holyrood, située à l'estrémité inférieure de la crête rocheuse longue d'un mile qui les sépare fut complété; la voie les reliant (le Royal Mile) se développa, formant l'axe principal de la vieille ville. Sa portion orientale, autrefois bourg indépendant, est encore connue sous le nom de Canongate.

Jeder Bürger dieser mittelalterlichen Stadt hatte sein eigenes Stück Land neben der High Street. Die Häuser waren strohgedeckte Fachwerkhäuser. Von den Zinnen der Burg erblickte man durch den Rauch der Holzfeuer die bewaldeten Hügel von „Arthurs Sitz". Jenseits der Felsenklüfte, wo Hirsche und Wildschweine sich ein Stelldichein gaben, wurde die Holyrood Abtei unter David, Margrets jüngstem Sohn, gegründet, die er um 1128 den Augustinern übergab.

Die Verbindung von Burg auf dem Fels und Abtei am Ende des meilenlangen Hügels war so hergestellt. Die Strecke zwischen Burg und Abtei, die sog. königliche Meile, gewann mehr und mehr an Bedeutung. Der östliche Teil hinter der Kreuzung von Jeffrey Street und St. Mary Street mit der High Street wird auf diesen Tag Canongate genannt und war einst ein unabhängiger Stadtteil.

The Guardian of the Growing City

In the twelfth century and up to the time of Bannockburn, the castle changed hands frequently. William I surrendered it to King Henry of England, but bought it back in a batch of castles for 10,000 silver merks from Henry's successor. Later, the now-strengthened fortress became the nation's repository for the national records – but these were destroyed by Edward I of England when he sacked the castle in 1291. Eventually, Bannockburn produced a temporary lull in this warring history and Edinburgh became a royal burgh in 1329. David II built a 60-foot fortified tower to strengthen the castle's defences and the settlement expanded into what is now the Grassmarket, southwards from the steep rocky foundations of the guardian fortress.

If the activities of the military were centred on the Castle Rock, the population's spiritual life centred on St Giles. Four great pillars within the building of today remain from around 1120, when a Norman church was erected to replace an even earlier construction. This survived till 1385, when Richard II of England devastated both town and church. Yet from the ashes rose what is essentially the building that stands today, complete with fifteenth-century crown spire. But in fourteenth-century Edinburgh, the thoughts of the citizens would too often have been filled with war and disorder, with weak monarchs at home and ambition in the English Court. Once again, in 1400, the castle was besieged, but patience from its

Below: St Giles Cathedral. *Right:* The Castle from the Vennel. *Below right:* The Canongate in the mid-nineteenth century

Ci-dessous: La Cathédrale St-Giles. *A droite:* Le Château, vu du « Vennel ». *Ci-dessous à droite:* « Canongate » au milieu de dix-neuvième siècle

Unten: St. Giles Kathedrale. *Rechts:* Das Schloß von der Vennel gesehen. *Unten rechts:* Canongate Mitte des 19. Jhs

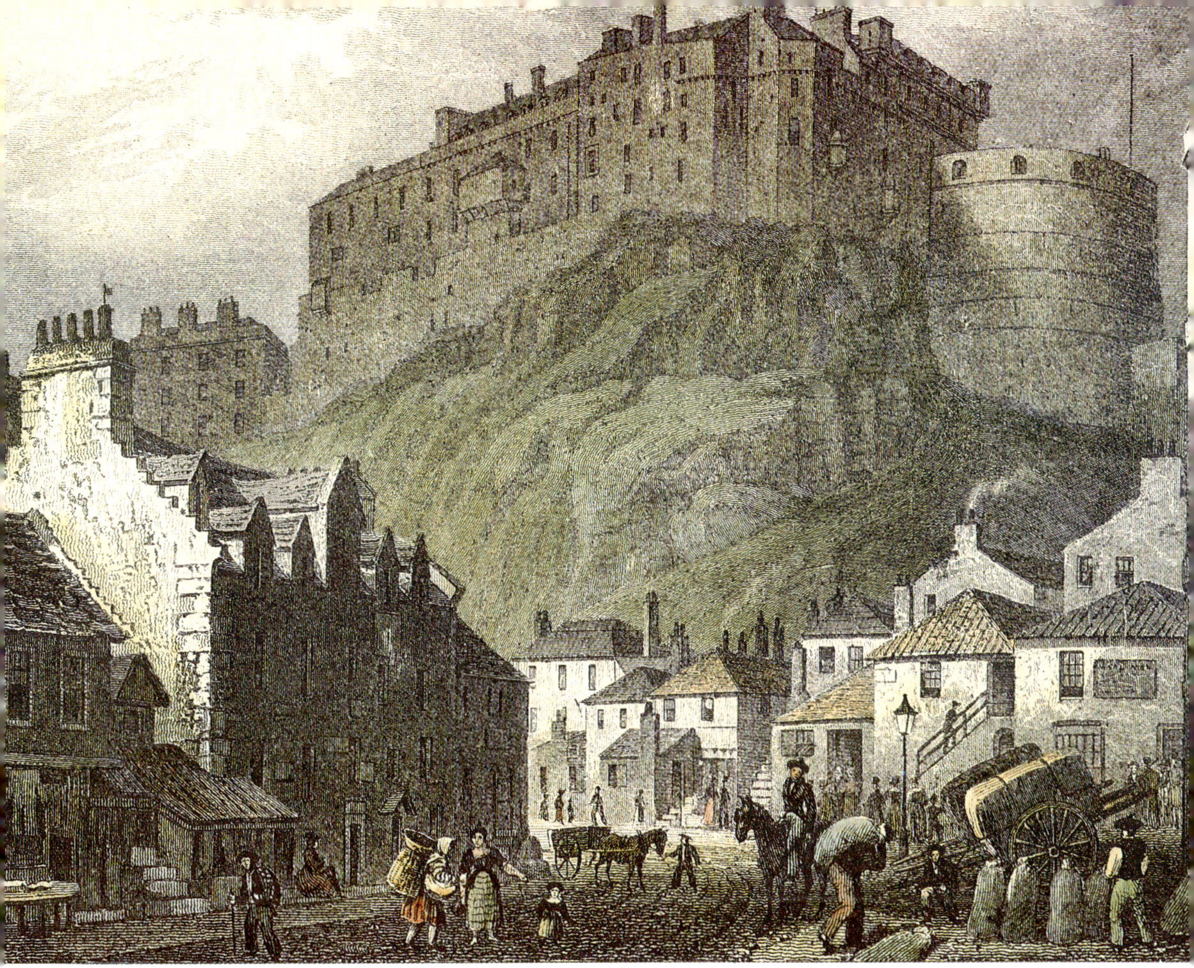

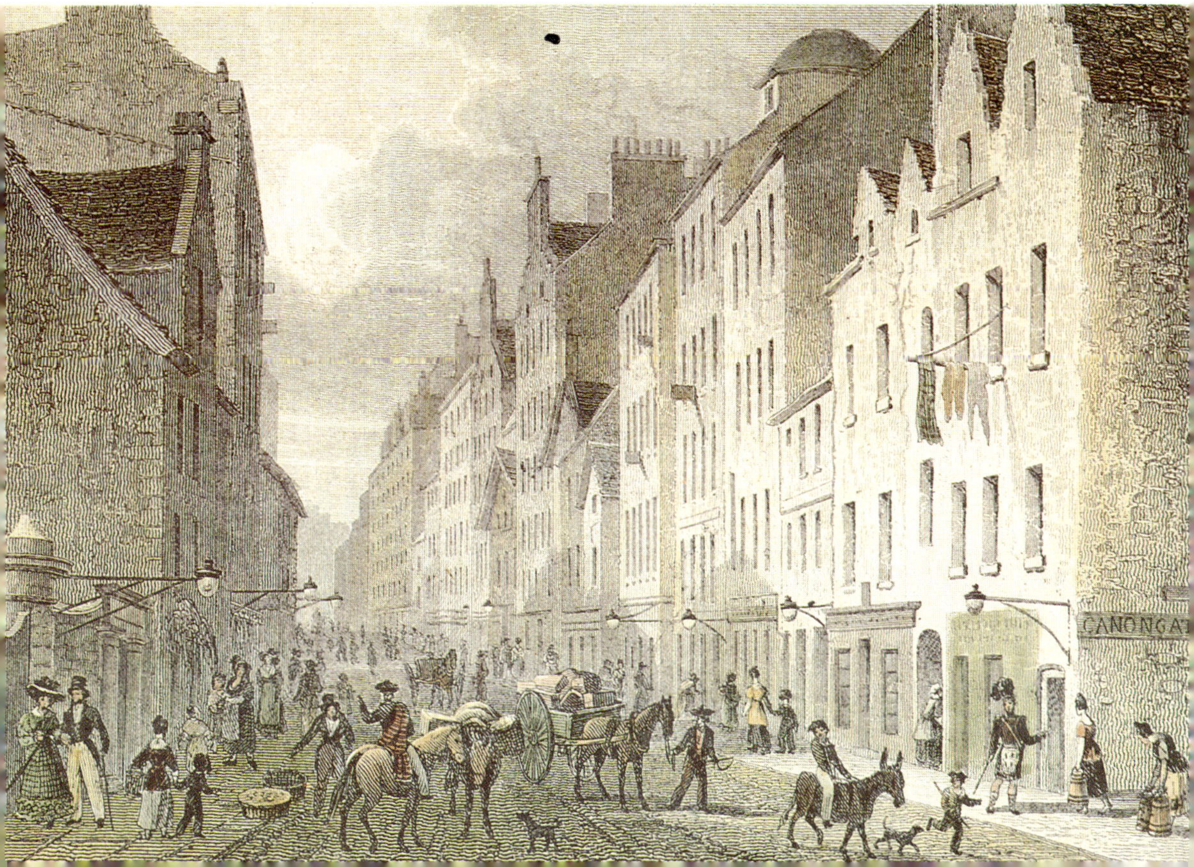
CANONGAT

defenders and the keen edged blade of a Scottish winter sent the invaders south.

Early fifteenth-century Edinburgh's population exceeded 2000 for the first time, many by this time housed in two-storey buildings of locally cut wood. The comparative stability during the reigns of the early Jameses was a time of consolidation. Edinburgh was by now the undisputed capital of the kingdom. A new city wall was sanctioned by James II. Fragments of this defensive structure remain at Castle Wynd which links Johnston Terrace and the Grassmarket, and at Tweeddale Court in the High Street. The swamp below the castle to the north was dammed, forming the Nor' Loch as a further defence. The citizens living in the Grassmarket and Cowgate areas were not at all happy with this arrangement. They were outside the defences and refused to contribute to the wall's costs.

On the Royal Mile meanwhile, the change from smallholdings to town houses was well under way – though the citizens did not altogether forsake their pastoral activities. Often the ground floor would be reserved for pigs or cattle. Access to the first floor was by an outside stair, as seen in the later Gladstone's Land today. As well as the completion of St Giles in 1495, another significant building nearby was the Tolbooth, which was to figure prominently in Edinburgh's civic life – as seat of the Scottish Parliament, Law Courts and prison. Today, only a heart-shape in stone set into the cobbles outside St Giles – an allusion to its role as a jail in Sir Walter Scott's *The Heart of Midlothian* – marks the site of this historic building which survived till 1817.

Lower down, while the Canongate attracted some buildings which reflected the prosperity of the Augustinian Canons, the medieval splendour of the Abbey of Holyrood was to be matched by a new palace – built to extend or replace the abbey's own guesthouse. In the early years of the sixteenth century James IV ordered the building of what is now the imposing north-west tower of Holyrood Palace – the oldest part of the façade seen today and one which has survived two fires: one a deliberate act of destruction by English invaders in 1544 and the second an accident in 1650. This fine tower with its adjoining new royal apartments fitted the brief splendour of the age – as did the jousting and pageantry held below the castle at the top end of the Royal Mile. West of the Grassmarket, in the close vicinity of the King's Stables Road of today, the knights paraded their skills before the Royal Court. But this time of relative peace was to end at Flodden, where the same Scottish knights who had performed gallantly in tournament were among the 10,000 who died in the rolling grassland of the Borders. The defensive wall subsequently thrown up around Edinburgh was known as the Flodden Wall. Parts of it, as well as subsequent additions, can be seen south of the Grassmarket. The western exit from the defences is echoed to this day in the West Port, running up and out of the Grassmarket, though the course of this sixteenth-century wall also ran much further to the east, below the site of the Royal Scottish Museum. Eventually, it turned back towards the Royal Mile, crossing it at the Netherbow Port, the most important town gate, at the St Mary Street/Jeffrey Street intersection with the High Street. Though his residence had become Holyrood Palace, the castle itself had been much improved by James IV. From this period dates the Great Hall, overlooking the sheer southern rocks.

Jusqu'en 1329, date à laquelle Edimbourg devint bourg royal, le château changea fréquemment de propriétaire. David II en renforça les défenses par la construction d'une tour fortifiée et la ville s'étendit au Sud vers le Grassmarket.

Si Castle Rock était le centre de l'activité militaire, l'église St Giles (1120) était celui de la vie spirituelle. Malgré un long et tumultueux passé (Richard II d'Angleterre dévasta la ville et l'église en 1385), l'édifice, reconstruit à la fin du 14ᵉ siècle, a survécu.

Avec plus de 2000 habitants, Edimbourg, désormais capitale indisputée du royaume, traversa au 15ᵉ siècle une période de paix et consolidation; un barrage transforma le marais au Nord de la ville en lac (Nor' Loch), formant, avec le nouveau mur d'enceinte construit sous Jacques II, des défenses supplémentaires.

A cette époque aussi les habitations bordant le Royal Mile peu à peu perdirent leur caractère agricole. En même temps que la nouvelle St Giles (terminée en 1495), s'élevait le Tolbooth, siège du parlement écossais, du palais de justice et de la prison. Cette con-

Opposite page, top: Interior Quadrangle, Holyrood Palace. *Opposite page, bottom left:* Telfer's Wall. *Opposite page, bottom right:* At Netherbow Port (now demolished). *Right:* Gladstone's Land

Ci-contre en haut: Cour intérieure, « Holyrood Palace ». *Ci-contre en bas à gauche:* « Telfer's Wall ». *Ci-contre en bas à droite:* Le port de Netherbow (aujourd'hui détruit). *A droite:* Le pays de Gladstone

Gegenüberliegende Seite, oben: viereckiger Innenhof, Holyrood Palast. *Gegenüberliegende Seite, unten links:* Telferswall. *Gegenüberliegende Seite, unten rechts:* Im Netherbow Hafen (heute abgerissen). *Rechts:* Gladstones Land

struction historique disparut en 1817; son emplacement est marqué par un pavé en forme de cœur situé près de St Giles.

Plus bas, le palais d'Holyrood vint rivaliser de splendeur avec l'abbaye. Au début du 16e siècle, Jacques IV ordonna la construction de l'imposante tour Nord-Ouest du palais, qui survécut à deux incendies (1544 et 1650).

Ces temps de paix relative se terminèrent brutalement à Flodden (1513), où les chevaliers qui autrefois prenaient part à d'élégants tournois, furent parmi les 10.000 victimes de cette terrible bataille, à la suite de laquelle d'autres remparts (Flodden Wall) furent érigés. On peut encore en voir quelques vestiges au Sud du Grassmarket. C'est de cette époque aussi que date le Great Hall qui surplombe la roche abrupte au Sud.

Die Burg wechselte vom 12. Jh. bis zur Zeit von Bannockburn häufig den Besitzer. Im Jahre 1329 erhielt Edinburgh königliches Statut. David II. erbaute einen Befestigungsturm und der gesamte Komplex erstreckte sich zum heutigen Grassmarket.

Anfang des 15. Jh. überschritt Edinburghs Einwohnerzahl die 2000 Grenze. Man lebte in zweistöckigen Holzhäusern. Unter der relativ friedlichen Herrschaft der ersten James setzte eine Zeit der Konsolidierung ein. Edinburgh war jetzt Hauptstadt des Königreiches. Eine lebhafte Bautätigkeit begann. James II. erbaute eine neue Stadtmauer, von der noch Reste bei Castle Wynd stehen.

Auf der königlichen Meile begann der Wandel von kleinen Bauernhöfen zu Stadthäusern, doch häufig blieb die untere Etage Stall für Kühe und Schweine. In den ersten Stock gelangte man mittels einer Außentreppe. St. Giles wurde 1495 vollendet. Ein weiteres bedeutendes Gebäude nahebei war Tolbooth, später Sitz des schottischen Parlamentes, Gericht und Gefängnis. Es überlebte bis 1817.

Weiter unten wurde der mittelalterliche Glanz der Holyrood Abtei mit dem Bau eines weiteren Palastes wiederholt. James IV. veranlaßte den Bau des Nordwestturmes des Holyrood Palastes, der heute einer der ältesten Fassaden darstellt und zwei Feuerbrünste überstanden hat. Dieser schöne Turm mit seinen angrenzenden königlichen Räumen entsprach dem kurzen Glanz dieser Zeit ebenso wie die Ritterturniere unterhalb der Burg am oberen Ende der königlichen Meile. Diese relativ friedliche und glanzvolle Zeit endete mit Flodden, wo dieselben Ritter unter den 10000 Kriegern waren, die auf den grünen Hügeln des Grenzlandes den Tod fanden. Von der Verteidigungsmauer, die danach um Edinburgh errichtet wurde, dem Floddenwall, sind noch heute Teile südlich des Grassmarket zu sehen.

The decades of the sixteenth century after Flodden were troubled times once again for the city, with the unstable minority of James V. Gavin Douglas, the king's tutor, poet and later Bishop of Dunkeld, once described himself as situated on 'the windy and richt unpleasant castell and royk of Edinburgh'. Though his comments on the prevailing meteorology are accurate enough, the castle's bravely exposed situation was enough to defeat an English army under the Earl of Hertford sent to burn the city in 1544 on the orders of Henry VIII. (James V had died and Henry was exercising a claim to the throne.) The invaders landed at Leith and left devastation in their wake. Yet with Holyrood ablaze, smoke and flame the length of the Royal Mile, the castle defences held secure.

Later, in 1566, Holyrood Palace was the scene of many acts in the drama of the most tragic Stuart monarch of all, Mary Queen of Scots. To this day, a plaque on the floor of a corridor marks the spot where her Italian secretary Rizzio fell with fifty wounds, her husband Darnley's dagger in his heart. History at this time is a dramatic interlocking of church and state. The Reformer John Knox had

Right: Old Edinburgh by Patrick and Alexander Nasmyth, 1822. Reproduced by courtesy of the Bank of Scotland, Edinburgh

A droite: Le vieil Edimbourg, de Patrick et Alexander Nasmyth, 1822

Rechts: Das alte Edinburgh von Patrick und Alexander Nasmyth, 1822

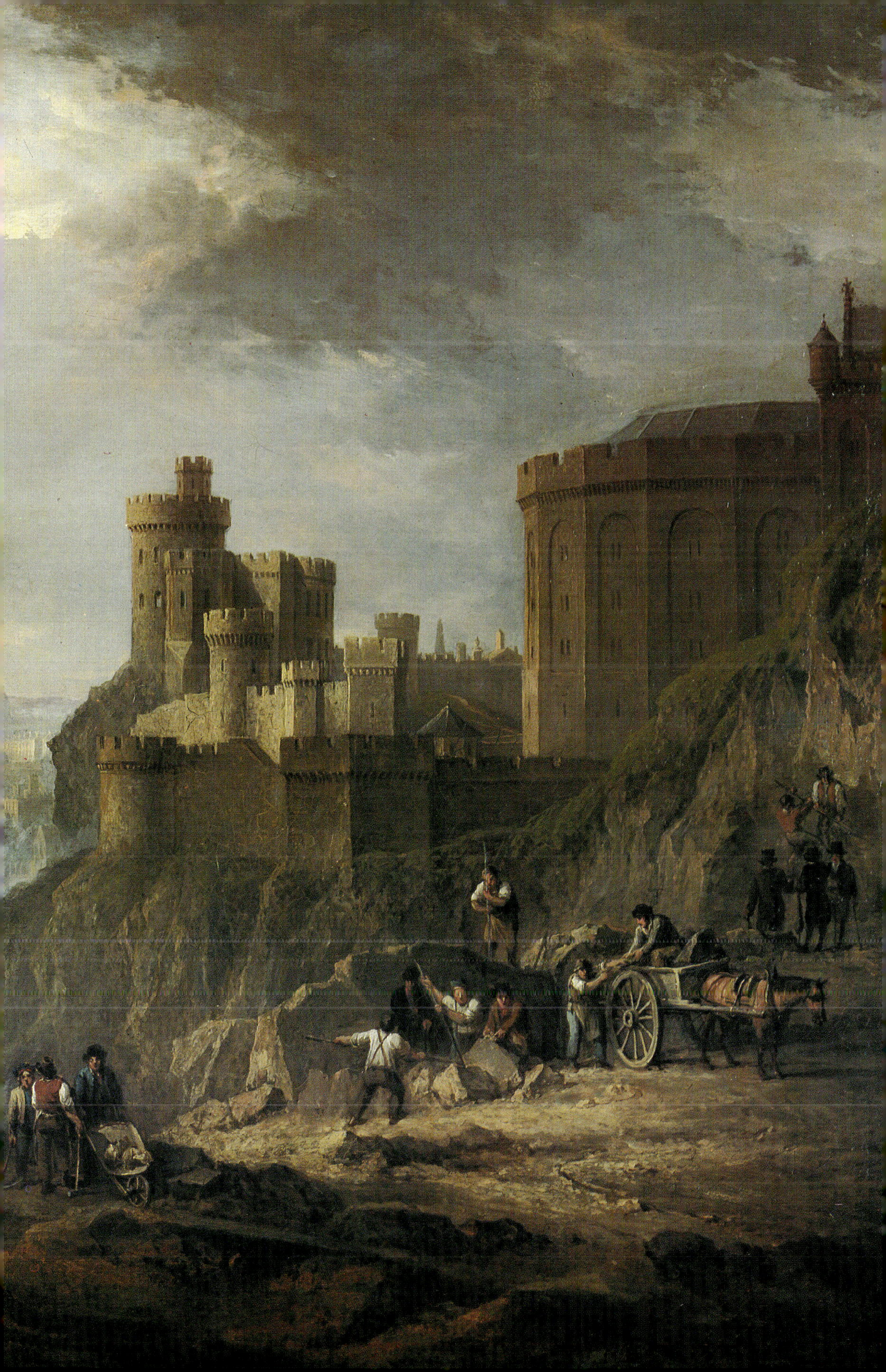

already preached his first sermon in St Giles by 1559, condemning the Old Church – yet one of Mary's first acts had been to attend Mass immediately after arriving in the capital in 1561. A bloody and complex chain of events subsequently unfolded; first Rizzio in Holyrood, then her husband Darnley was found dead after an unexplained explosion in the Kirk o' Field, a collegiate house near the Cowgate. There followed the strange, brief marriage to Bothwell. In this tangled drama, ambitious nobles, religious conflict, and the fatal charm of this unhappy monarch meant that even after many twists to the tale and her eventual removal as a prisoner to Loch Leven Castle, the capital was to witness further violence. Some factions rallied to Mary's support and, under Sir James Kirkcaldy of Grange, held out in Edinburgh Castle for six years. Eventually, Queen Elizabeth of England sent heavy guns to support the attackers, led by the Regent Morton. These huge field-pieces, firing from what is now Princes Street on one side, as well as from the vicinity of Lothian Road and George Heriot's School, finally brought down David's Tower (built in 1356). Men, guns and masonry crashed down 200 feet to the Nor' Loch. Next, the Spur was captured, on what is now the Esplanade and with it the chief water supply to the fortress. The most destructive siege in the castle's history ended in 1573. On this battered slope, the Half Moon Battery was subsequently built on instructions from the Regent Morton.

La ville connut de nouveau une période troublée après Flodden sous le règne de Jacques V. A la mort de celui-ci, en 1544, une armée du roi Henri VIII ayant mission de dévaster la ville, mit le feu à Holyrood et le long du Royal Mile; les défenses du château cependant tinrent bon.

Holyrood fut également le témoin de scènes tragiques de l'histoire du plus romanesque souverain d'Ecosse, Marie Stuart. Une plaque marque encore l'emplacement où son secrétaire italien, Rizzio, tomba de cinquante blessures, dont l'une au moins causée par le poignard de l'époux de la reine, Darnley. Celui-ci succomba aussi peu après et le mariage de la reine à Bothwell à quelque temps de là causa scandale, comme le firent ses opinions religieuses. Après l'emprisonnement de Marie Stuart à Loch Leven et son abdication, Edimbourg connut encore de violentes altercations entre partisans de la reine et ceux de sa rivale d'Angleterre, Elisabeth I^e. Ces derniers eurent finalement gain de cause en 1573, après un siège de 6 ans.

Die letzten Jahre des 16. Jhs. nach Flodden waren für die Stadt wieder turbulente Zieten unter der Herrschaft des minderjährigen James V. mit Angriffen auf Stadt und Burg. Holyrood und die gesamte königliche Meile standen in Flammen, die Burg jedoch hielt trotzig stand.

Später im Jahre 1566 war der Holyrood Palast Schauplatz für die tragischste Figur der Stuart Monarchen, Maria Stuart. Eine Tafel im Fußboden eines der Korridore erinnert an die Stelle, an der ihr italienischer Sekretär Rizzio den fünfzig Dolchstößen ihres Gemahles Darnley erlag. Die Geschichte dieser Zeit zeigt eine dramatische Verquickung von Staat und Kirche. Der Reformator John Knox verdammte in seiner Predigt in St. Giles 1559 die alte katholische Kirche. Marias erste Amtshandlung jedoch war es, nach ihrer Ankunft in der Stadt 1561 sofort in die Messe zu gehen. Nach Rizzios Ermordung wurde ihr Gemahl in einer unerklärlichen Explosion getötet. Danach folgte die merkwürdige Heirat mit Bothwell. Ehrgeizige Adlige, religiöse Konflikte und ihr großer Charme wurden der Königin zun Verhängnis und führten zum Ausbruch von Gewalt in der Stadt. Manche parteien eilten zu ihrer Unterstützung und verbarrikadierten sich unter Führung von Sir James Kircaldy von Grange sechs Jahre lang in der Burg. Königin Elizabeth I. schickte schließlich schwere Kanonen für die Angreifer. Der 1356 erbaute Davidturm fiel unter dem Angriff. Die Belagerung endete 1573 mit dem Sieg der Angreifer.

City Life Below the Battlements

As Edinburgh's story moves on towards the seventeenth century, buildings which survive today echo these dramatic times. They remind the visitor of the continuity of domestic and commercial life, regardless of political upheavals. Much of the structure of Riddle's Court still stands, built by a burgess on the Lawnmarket within a few years of the drama of the siege. Again, in the troubled reign of Mary, John Knox himself may have lived further down the High Street in the dwelling now named after him – though more definite is the evidence that it was the home of Mary Queen of Scots' goldsmith, James Mossman – his initials decorate the outside. This outstanding example of the city's domestic architecture may go back to 1490 – a survivor of Hertford's raid, mentioned above – while its neighbour, Moubray House, claims 1472 as its earliest possible building date – thus it was well over 200 years old when Daniel Defoe, journalist and novelist, edited the Edinburgh Courant from it in the early eighteenth century.

Further down the Mile, in the Canongate, another Tolbooth was built, as befitted the status of the independent burgh. Opposite still stands Huntly House, which started life as domestic dwellings sometime in the sixteenth century. It is now a museum of local life. This settlement was to prosper particularly after 1603 and the Union of the Crowns. James VI of Scotland became James I of England and, in its own domestic way, Canongate collectively gave a sigh of relief – it was, after all, still outside the city wall. With the prospect of a lasting peace, the little burgh built more spacious dwellings. Moray House, dating from around 1635, is now a teacher training college; once it was the sumptuous home of a dowager.

Up the hill and through the Netherbow Port, where the city proper began, building continued in a high-rise mode. This eastern route, through residential development on the Royal Mile, was in contrast to the western approach to the city, by the West Port, that led through the Grassmarket, with its decidedly commercial flavour. A weekly market was held there in accordance with a charter originally granted by King James III in 1477 and this custom survived until 1911. On a more sinister note, the Grassmarket was also the place of public executions, the gallows site still marked by a cross in the cobbles and a small fenced-off garden area. Before a much later reconstruction, West Bow, confusingly at the east end of the Grassmarket, gave direct access to Castle Hill and the Lawnmarket, this last part in former times hazardous, colourful and noisy with the numerous stalls of the lawn-merchants, displaying their bales of cloth to all passers-by. These sellers of cloth also shared this area with traders in other domestic produce – wool, butter, cheese – weighed at the Old Butter Tron which occupied the Lawnmarket/Johnston Terrace junction site till 1660.

With the Cowgate running parallel in the valley south of the main ridge of the Royal Mile, this comparatively straightforward city plan comprised all of Edinburgh. The wealthy burgesses living on the upper floors of the tall dwellings on the Mile and the stall owners whose 'luckenbooths' occupied the ground floor, can truly be said to have seen much of Scotland's history happen in this little area. They would have witnessed the near-riot spilling out of St Giles in response to readings from a new prayer book, part of the Anglican

Opposite: The Kirk o' Field. *Below: Edinburgh from the top of Princes Street* by Gendall Sutherland. By courtesy of Edinburgh City Libraries.

Ci-contre: L'église o' Field. *Ci-dessous: Edimbourg, du haut de « Princes Street »,* de Gendall Sutherland

Gegenüber: Kirk o Field. *Unten: Blick auf Edinburgh vom oberen Teil der Princes Street* her gesehen von Gendall Sutherland

reforms promoted by Charles I. To the congregation that day in 1637, they smacked too much of Catholicism. Soon this feeling had crystallised into the National Covenant, not simply an affirmation of belief in a free parliament, but a full-scale political statement which challenged the rights of the Crown itself. Soon Edinburgh Castle, like other Royalist forts in the country, was under attack by Covenanting forces. Though Edinburgh was only a part of the broad canvas on which the events of the next twelve years were painted, the watching citizens on the Royal Mile were to see James Graham of Montrose, Lieutenant-General of the king, hanged 30 feet above the Mercat Cross, near St Giles – then, after the king's own execution, they witnessed Cromwell himself marching in to take possession in 1650. In this troubled and confused time, Parliament House had just been completed, behind St Giles, though for a glimpse of its original architecture, the visitor must peer at its Scots Gothic style and rubble stonework from George IV Bridge, near the National Library.

The children of these same denizens of the Mile would have

Opposite page, top: John Knox's Corner and the Old Exchequer by Mrs J. Stewart Smith, 1867. By courtesy of Edinburgh City Libraries. *Opposite page, bottom:* White Horse Close by T. Webb, 1823. By courtesy of Edinburgh City Libraries. *This page, top:* Moray House in the Canongate. *This page, bottom:* The Grassmarket, looking West

Ci-contre en haut: « John Knox's Corner » et « Old Exchequer », de Mme J. Stewart Smith, 1867. *Ci-contre en bas:* « White Horse Close », de T. Webb, 1823. *Cette page en haut:* « Moray House » dans « Canongate ». *Cette page en bas:* « The Grassmarket », en direction de l'Ouest

Gegenüberliegende Seite, oben: John Knox Ecke und das Alte Schatzamt von Mrs. J. Stewart Smith, 1867. *Gegenüberliegende Seite, unten:* Weiße Roßgasse von T. Webb, 1823. *Diese Seite, oben:* Moray Haus in Canongate. *Diese Seite, unten:* Der Grasmarkt gen Westen

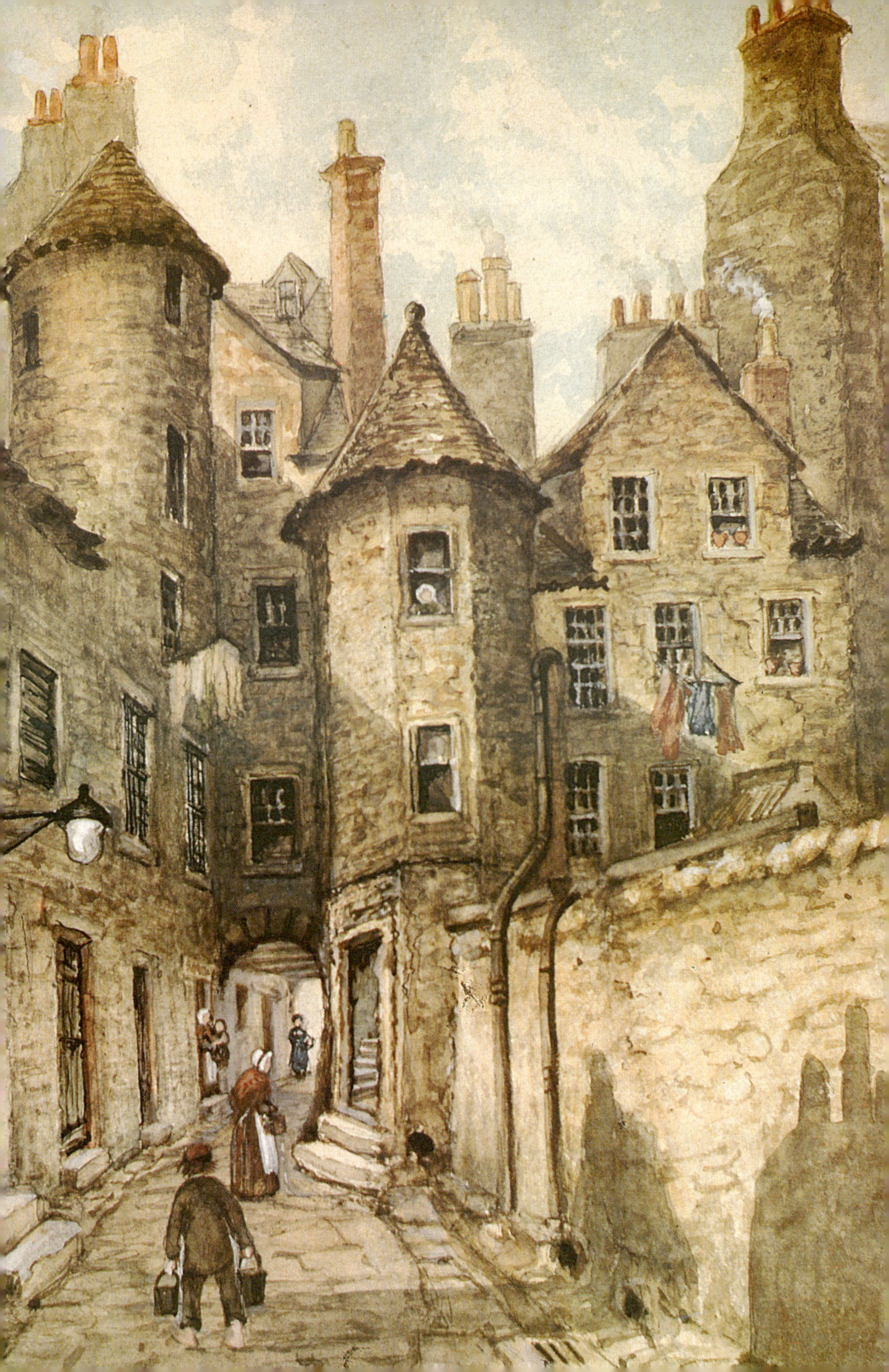

witnessed a waterspout, near the Mercat Cross, running with wine, when Restoration celebrations in 1660 marked the return of a king – Charles II – to the throne. Mons Meg, the great cannon still to be seen in the castle, boomed out its approval, and army and citizens alike marched with drums boldly beating from the Lawnmarket down to Holyrood Palace.

But babes in arms on that day would later have seen, as solid and respectable middle-aged merchants, perhaps, a procession pass the other way. Scotland had lost her independence. In 1707 the last 'riding of parliament' took place. Plumed horses and the glinting trumpeters would no longer pass solemnly in splendour en route for Parliament House.

But peace was not yet at hand. The indirect rule from London which followed the ending of Scotland's own parliament would have been one element in the mood of anger that erupted in the famous Porteous Riot in 1736, but this domestic incident was on a much smaller scale than the events of 1745. Edinburgh played host to Prince Charles Edward Stuart and his forces for six weeks. Ironically, the castle garrison itself held out for the Government and on the last day of October, some unknown soldier must have loaded the last round ever to be fired in deadly earnest. The prince had left the city, heading for England and ultimately final defeat at Culloden.

L'histoire d'Edimbourg se reflète aussi dans son architecture domestique dont nous sont parvenus Riddle's Court (1490) et Moubray House (1472), célèbre pour avoir hébergé, 200 ans plus tard, l'écrivain Daniel Defoe.

Opposite: St John's Close, Canongate by Mrs J. Stewart Smith, 1867. By courtesy of Edinburgh City Libraries. Above left: St Giles Cathedral. Below: The Castle, Ramsay Gardens, Bank of Scotland and the Earthen Mound from Princes Street

Ci-contre: « St-John's Close », « Canongate », de Mme J. Stewart Smith, 1867. Ci-dessus à gauche: La Cathédrale St-Giles. Ci-dessous: Le Château, « Ramsay Gardens », « Bank of Scotland » et « Earthen Mound » de « Princes Street »

Gegenüber: St. John Gasse, Canongate von Mrs. J. Stewart Smith, 1867. Oben links: St. Giles Kathedrale. Unten: Das Schloß, Ramsay Gärten, die Bank von Schottland und der Erdhügel von Princes Street gesehen

Plus bas, dans Canongate, un autre Tolbooth fait face à Huntley House, maison bourgeoise devenue musée d'histoire locale et située non loin de Moray House.

Alors qu'à l'Est du Royal Mile un quartier résidentiel se développait, l'Ouest de la ville, et en particulier le Grassmarket (où un marché hebdomadaire se tint jusqu'en 1911) était marqué par les activités commerciales. Grassmarket était aussi le lieu des exécutions publiques (l'emplacement du gibet est marqué par une croix dans les pavés). Tout près de là, Lawnmarket abritait le marché aux étoffes, ainsi que le commerce de la laine, du beurre et du fromage.

L'ancienne cité d'Edimbourg est presque entièrement comprise entre le Royal Mile et Cowgate et c'est là aussi que se déroulèrent la plus grande partie des événements historiques qui devaient suivre.

Au 17ᵉ siècle, les querelles religieuses dégénérèrent en guerre civile et le National Covenant alla jusqu'à remettre en question les droits de la couronne elle-même.

Edimbourg, comme d'autres villes du royaume, fut le témoin des batailles entre royalistes et covenanters au cours des douze années qui suivirent.

1660 vit la restauration, fêtée dans la liesse, mais en 1707 l'Ecosse ayant perdu son indépendance, le parlement y défila pour la dernière fois.

Edimbourg connut encore des époques troublées, notamment les rébellions contre la couronne d'Angleterre en 1736, et, plus particulièrement, en 1745, la tentative de Bonnie Prince Charlie de reprendre le trône d'Ecosse, aventure qui se termina tragiquement pour lui et ses partisans à la bataille de Culloden en 1746.

Viele der alten Gebäude der Stadt weisen Spuren ihrer dramatischen Vergangenheit auf. Das Gebäude Riddle's Court wurde einige Jahre nach der Belagerung erbaut, etwa um 1490. Vermutlich hat John Knox in dem nach ihm benannten Gebäude auf der High Street gelebt, aber noch eher ist anzunehmen, daß es das Haus von James Mossman, dem Goldschmied Maria Stuarts war, denn seine Initialen schmücken die Hausfront. Moubray House daneben rühmt sich eines noch früheren Baudatums, nämlich 1472. Daniel Defoe, Journalist und Schriftsteller, gab von hier seine Zeitschrift, die Edinburgh Courant, heraus. Das war Anfang des 18. Jhs. Weitere historische, interessante Gebäude auf der Meile sind Huntly House, heute Museum und Moray House, heute pädagogische Hochschule.

Den Hügel hinauf und durch das Netherbow Tor begann die eigentliche Stadt. Diese östliche Route stand mit ihrem Wohnviertelcharakter im Gegensatz zum westlichen Zugang durch das Westtor mit ausgesprochenem kommerziellen Charakter. Hier wurde bis 1911 Wochenmarkt abgehalten. Der Grassmarket war Galgenplatz, wo öffentliche Hinrichtungen stattfanden. Ein kleiner, eingezäunter Garten mit einem Kreuz auf dem Pflaster zeigt

des Jahres 1637 erschienen diese der Gemeinde wohl zu katholisch. Von hier kam es bald zum Nationalabkommen, in dem sich nicht nur der Wunsch nach einem freien Parlament niederschlug, sondern in dem auch die Rechte der Krone infrage gestellt wurden. Die Edinburgher Burg und andere königliche Festungen wurden von den Anhängern des Nationalabkommens belagert. Wiederum wurden die Bürger der königlichen Meile Zeugen der Gewalt und des Blutvergiessens. James Graham of Montrose, des Königs General, wurde nahe St. Giles aufgehängt, später im Jahre 1650 nach Hinrichtung des Königs, sahen sie Cromwell einmarschieren. Während dieser gewalttätigen Zeit war das parlamentsgebäude hinter St. Giles vollendet worden.

Die Kinder derselben Bürger sahen, während der Festlichkeiten anläßlich der Rückkehr Charles II. auf den Thron, eine Fontäne Wein speien. Das war im Jahre 1660. Die nächste Generation sah Schottland seine Unabhängigkeit verlieren. Im Jahr 1707 fand zum letzten Mal dern von Prunk und Glanz begleitete Einzug ins Parlament statt.

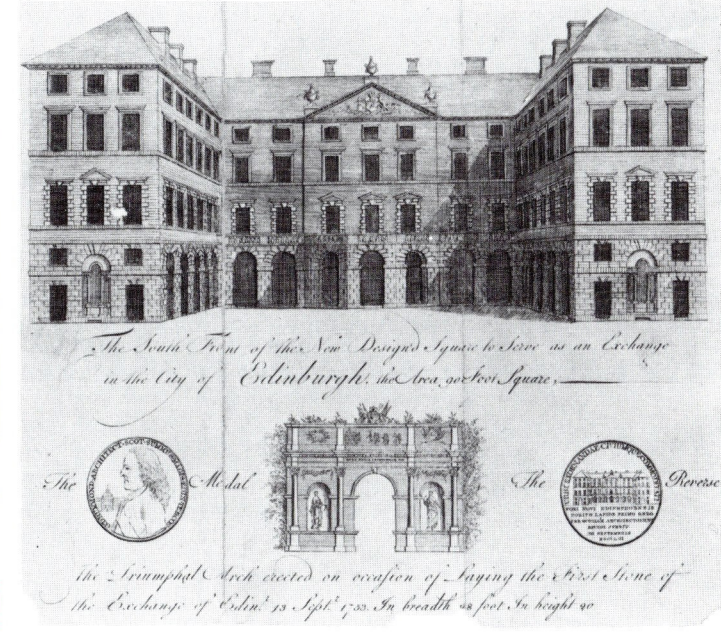

Above: The Tolbooth. *Above right:* Design drawings of the Royal Exchange. *Below right:* George Square

Ci-dessus: Le « Tolbooth ». *Ci-dessus à droite:* Plans du « Royal Exchange ». *Ci-dessous à droite:* « George Square »

Oben: Tolbooth. *Oben rechts:* Entwurfsskizzen der Königlichen Börse. *Unten rechts:* George Square

heute die Stelle des Galgens an.

Die wohlhabenden Bürger der königlichen Meile lebten im oberen Stock ihrer Häuser. Im Untergeschoß waren ladeninhaber, die wohl auf kleinstem Raum einen guten Teil schottischer Geschichte wahrgenommen haben müssen. Sie waren vielleicht Zeugen für den Fast-Aufruhr vor St. Giles, weil während des Gottesdienstes aus dem neuen Gebetsbuch gelesen worden war, welches einen Teil der von Charles I. eingeführten Reformen darstellte. An diesem Tag

A New Town Beyond the Castle

Fletcher of Saltoun, the Scottish patriot, wrote as far back as 1698: 'As the happy situation of LONDON has been the principal cause of the glory and riches of ENGLAND; so the bad situation of EDINBURGH, has been one great occasion of the poverty and uncleanliness in which the greater part of the people of SCOTLAND live.' He was right – stories of the filth and squalor of Scotland's capital by writers from medieval times onwards are hardly exaggerated. How could it be otherwise with the great density of dwellings without proper sanitation confined in such a small space? By 1760, when George III came to the throne, the population stood at about 50,000, with some writers estimating that around a tenth of that figure were destitute and homeless.

But improvements were beginning to take place. Several ruinous tenements in the High Street were demolished and a grand new Royal Exchange rose to completion by 1761. (The excavated material from its foundations was used to construct the Castle Esplanade.) This imposing building is now the City Chambers. By 1766, George Square, to the south, had been built as a speculative development. In spite of subsequent and somewhat unbalanced redevelopment by the University, enough remains for the visitor to imagine the fashionable and 'modern' housing that attracted the aristocratic and the well-to-do – including Walter Scott W.S., a successful lawyer with a soon-to-be-famous son. However, it was the lands to the north that were to alter most dramatically, with the creation of the now famous 'New Town'.

Between the old city and the sea was a low ridge where an ancient road called the Lang Dykes ran (now roughly occupied by George Street). Visions of a new city of open spaces and fine proportions – as well as economic advantages – resulted in the announcement of a competition for the design of a 'New Town'. The eventual winner was a young, unknown architect called James Craig. His plan of 1767 was simple – a grid-iron of symmetrical streets, squares and gardens.

By this time, draining of the Nor' Loch was well under way. This was necessary to create firm foundations for the North Bridge, the means of access to the new ground to the north, which, it seems, had already been bought by city officials with an eye for a quick profit should the development prove successful.

One of the first major buildings

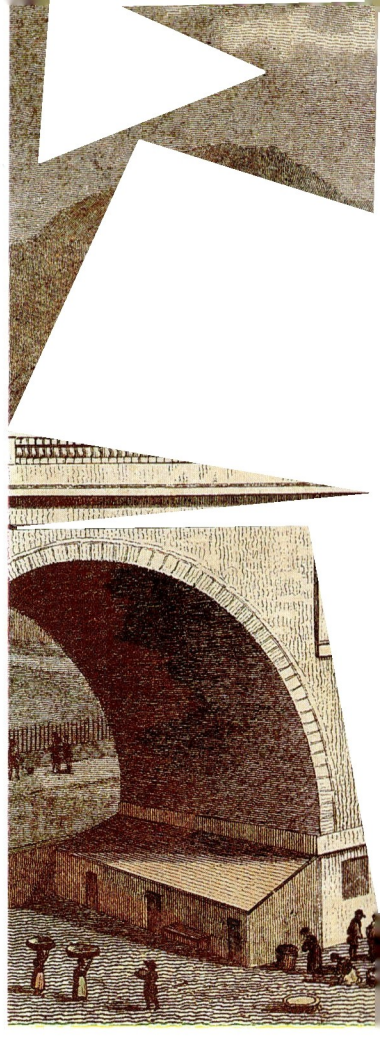

in the New Town was Register House, designed by Robert and James Adam and completed in 1788. Conceived as the Public Record Office for the nation, part of the money to build it came from the revenues of forfeited Jacobite estates – that is, from the lands of those chiefs who had fought on the wrong side at Culloden in 1746. The late eighteenth century stroller would have had a good view of Register House from the North Bridge. Now, the twentieth-century hubbub of traffic at the junction of North Bridge and Princes Street, the flocks of carrier-bag laden citizens and the close proximity of more recent architecture all combine to prevent the visitor stepping back to admire its fine proportions.

While the tide of development rolled onwards and over the Cowgate via a new South Bridge, opened in 1788, the symmetry and grand simplicity of Craig's plan continued to take shape to the north in well-cut ashlar and cast railings. St Andrew's Square was completed by 1781, with streets eastwards well under way, although one of the square's most interesting buildings, that of the Royal Bank of Scotland on the east side, does not conform to Craig's plan. This was originally the mansion of the wealthy and influential Sir Lawrence Dundas. Some historians have suggested that he must have known of Craig's, and hence the authorities', plan for a church at each end of the two squares (St Andrew's and Charlotte) but was so determined to build his own property that he managed – somehow – to overlook, or perhaps suppress, the fact that a religious building was intended for 'his' site. A consequence of this was the siting of St Andrew's Church, completed in 1787, in George Street. Its interior in particular is considered a triumph of neo-classical simplicity and harmony.

The view across to the castle and the open, airy and dramatic situation of Princes Street were preserved for today's visitors only after a long-drawn out and heated legal battle which took place towards the end of the eighteenth century between owners of property on the north side of the famous thoroughfare and speculative developers – with the Town Council of the day siding with the speculators. The matter went as far

Above: The North Bridge before the railway was built beneath it. *Left:* Register House

Ci-dessus: « North Bridge » avant la construction, sous celui-ci, du chemin de fer. *A gauche:* « Register House »

Oben: Die Nordbrücke vor Erbauung der Eisenbahnlinie darunter. *Links:* Register House

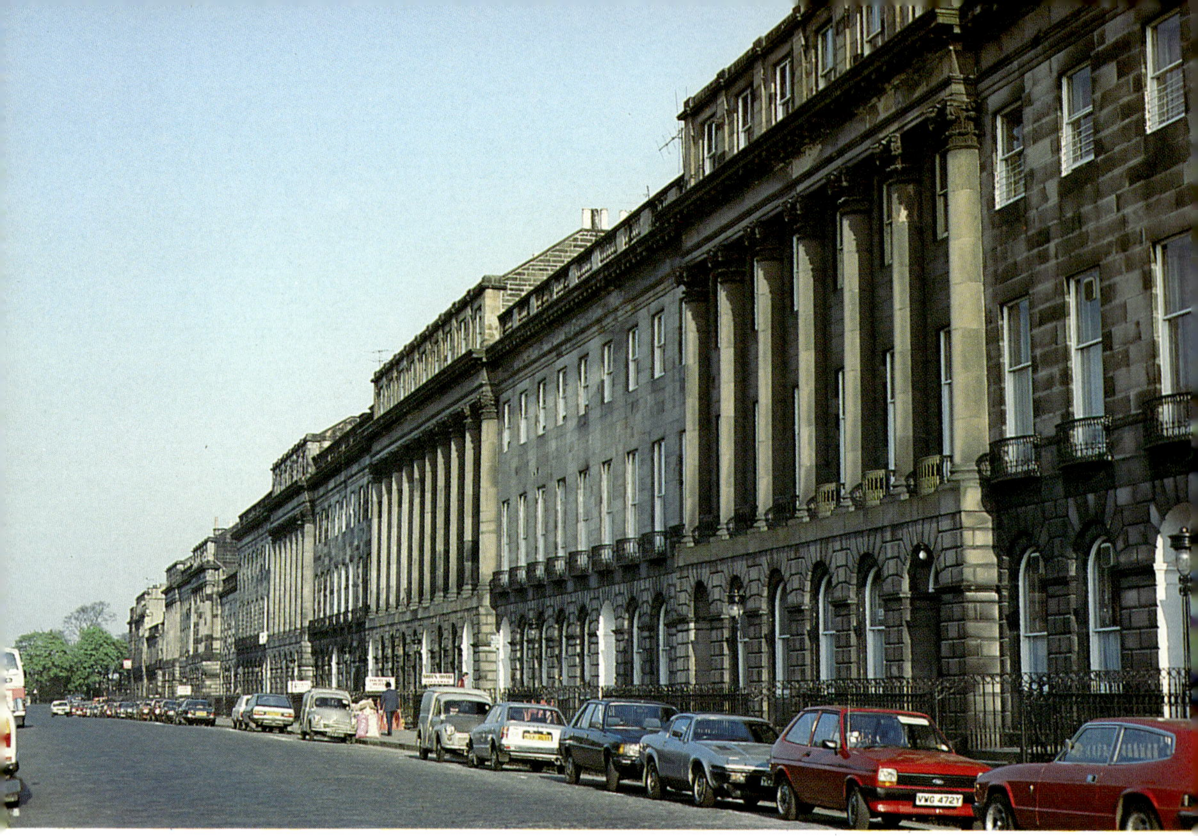
VWG 472Y

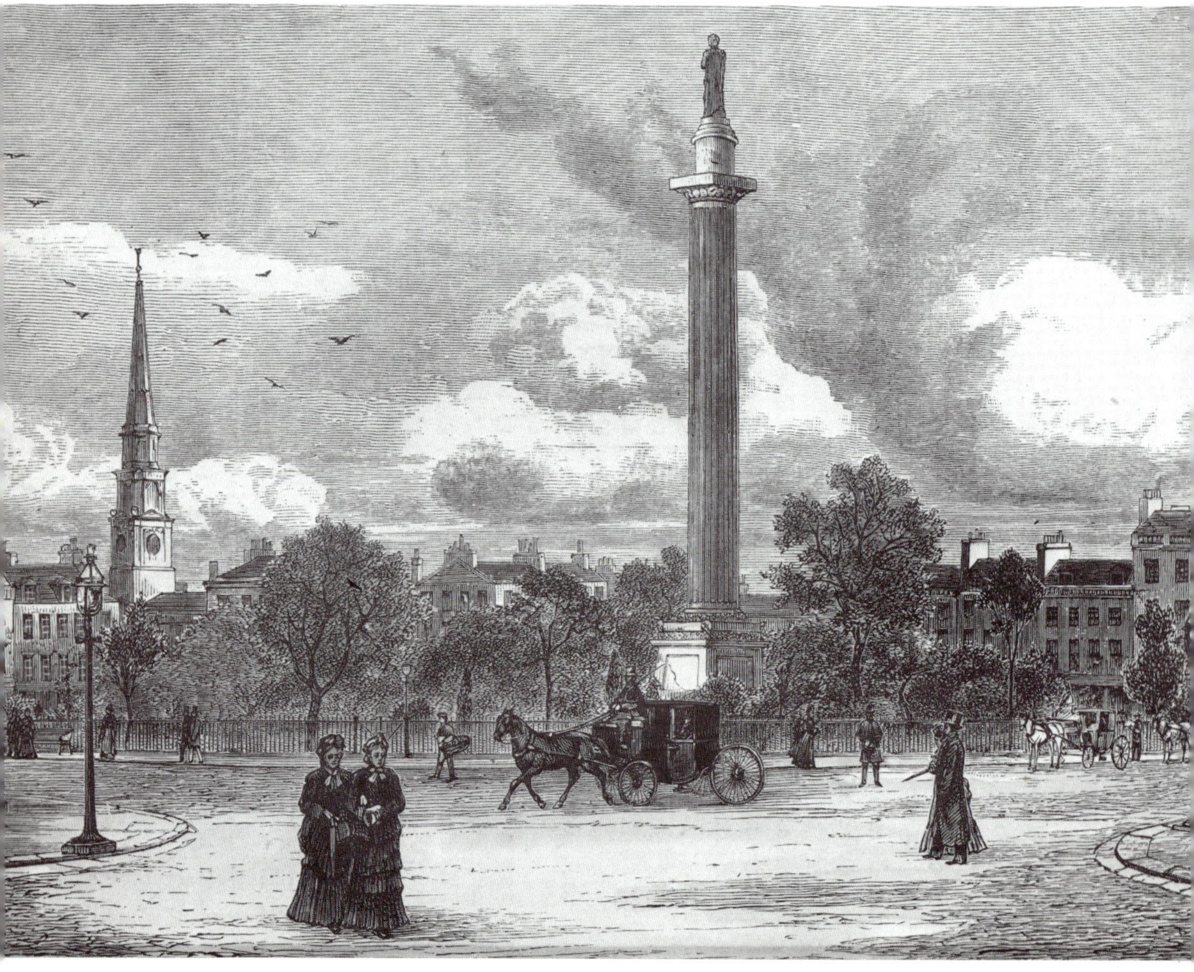

as the House of Lords – indicating that the owners of houses on Princes Street in those days were certainly men of substance. The shape of the street even today is evidence of the compromise that was finally reached – the new Waverley Market is decidedly low-profile, while westwards, there are no buildings on the south side apart from the Scott Monument and the façade of the Royal Scottish Academy – to which not even the ghosts of those first weighty residents could object.

As the building of the grid continued westwards in the last twenty years of the eighteenth century, the town council turned its attention to Charlotte Square. With the eventual execution of most of the plan by Robert Adam, this part of the city was to receive praise as one of the finest examples of civic architecture to be seen anywhere in Europe. Still largely intact to this day (if intrusive dormer windows in places are discounted, not to mention considerable 'tinkering' with the original Adam design for the whole square), the north side in particular with its 'palace' frontage is spectacularly successful. It is entirely appropriate that the National Trust for Scotland have made No. 7 a memorial to this elegant age. 'The Georgian House' is furnished throughout in late eighteenth-century style and open to the public.

L'Edimbourg médiévale était connue pour la pauvreté de ses habitants et ses conditions insalubres; vers 1760, la ville comptait 50.000 habitants, dont un dixième au moins vivait dans la misère totale.

Une amélioration cependant se fit jour en 1761 avec la démolition de taudis dans la High Street et la construction de l'imposant Royal Exchange. Vers 1766, un ensemble d'habitations « modernes » se développa autour de George Square, pour la population aristocratique de la ville. Mais c'est surtout au Nord de la ville que se bâtit la célèbre « ville nouvelle », sur les terrains situés entre la vieille ville et la mer. Un jeune architecte inconnu, James Craig, remporta le concours lancé pour la conception de la « ville nouvelle », avec un plan simple en forme de grille régulière avec squares et jardins. Le Nor' Loch fut également asséché.

Register House, destinée à contenir les archives écossaises et bâtie

Above left: Royal Terrace. *Above centre:* St Andrew's Church in George Street. *Above right:* Princes Street in the second half of the nineteenth century. *Left:* St Andrew's Square

Ci-dessus à gauche: « Royal Terrace ». *Ci-dessus au centre:* L'église St-Andrew dans « George Street ». *Ci-dessus à droite:* « Princes Street » pendant la deuxième moitié du dix-neuvième siècle. *A gauche:* « St-Andrew's Square »

Oben links: Königliche Terrasse. *Oben Mitte:* St. Andrew Kirche in der George Straße. *Oben rechts.* Princes Street in der zweiten Hälfte des 19. Jhs. *Links:* St. Andrew's Square

surti les plans de Robert et James Adam, fut complétée en 1788. Tandis que la ville se développait aussi vers le Sud avec la construction de South Bridge en 1788, la « ville nouvelle » s'agrandissait. St Andrew's Square fut terminé en 1781, comprenant entre autres l'immeuble de la Royal Bank of Scotland construit à l'emplacement prévue par Craig pour une église (St Andrew's). Celle-ci (terminée en 1787) et située dans George Street, est généralement considérée comme un exemple brillant de l'architecture georgienne (néo-classique). La « ville nouvelle » se poursuivit aussi vers l'Ouest, avec en particulier Charlotte Square sur les plans de Robert Adam, universellement considéré comme l'une des merveilles d'architecture domestique d'Europe. Le No. 7 a été transformé en musée.

Vom Mittelalter an erwähnten Schriftsteller und Dichter immer wieder Edinburghs Schmutz und Elend, was kaum zu verwundern war, wenn man sich die auf kleinstem Raum zusammengedrängten Gebäude ohne jegliche Sanitation vor Augen führt. Um 1760 mit Georg III. auf dem Thron betrug die Einwohnerzahl der Stadt 50000, von denen nach Ansicht mancher ein Zehntel bedürftig und odachlos waren.

Doch bald setzten Verbesserungen ein. Einige Gebäude in der High Street wurden abgerissen und machten der großartigen, königlichen Börse Platz. Um 1766 wurden die Häuser um George Square erbaut. Noch heute kann man sich vorstellen, wie attraktiv diese damals modernen Häuser für die Aristokraten und Wohlsituierten gewesen sein müssen.

Zwischen der alten Stadt und der See verlief ein niedriger Grat mit einer Landstraße, der Lang Dykes. Heute nimmt George Street ihren Platz ein. Schon lange hatte man die Vorstellung von einer neuen Stadt mit Raum, Licht und schönen Proportionen. Dies führte dann zu einem Preisausschreiben mit dem Entwurf einer „neuen Stadt". Gewinner wurde ein junger, unbekannter Architekt namens James Craig. Sein Plan war einfach — ein gitterartiges Netz symmetrisch verlaufender Straßen,

Plätze und Gärten.

Das Nor' Loch wurde trockengelegt, um ein solides Fundament für den Bau der Nordbrücke zu schaffen, die den Zugang vom Norden zur neuen Stadt ermöglichte.

Eines der ersten großen Gebäude in der Neustadt war Register House von Robert und James Adam entworfen und 1788 erbaut. St. Andrew's Square wurde 1781 beendet. Die Stadtväter konzentrierten ihre Aufmerksamkeit auf Charlotte Square. Nach dem Plan von Robert Adam entstanden in diesem Teil der Stadt mit die schönsten städtischen Gebäude Europas.

Ironically, just as the intended church at St Andrew's Square was misplaced, there were also some difficulties with the religious building on Charlotte Square. The Town Council did not adopt

Religion aside, perhaps the atmosphere in the early part of the 'New Town' seems a little severe – though this interpretation is doubtless influenced by meteorological as much as architectural factors, as any visitor tacking up Princes Street in a moist south-westerly would agree.

Less prone to sudden chills from exposed corners is the second phase of the 'New Town'. The land falls gently away with a north exposure from the now built-up Lang Dykes, that is, George Street, and by the 1820s the sound of masons' hammers was heard from the valley of the Water of Leith in the west almost to the edge of the Calton Hill. William Playfair was the architect of the wooded, sheltered crescents of Royal Circus. Moray Place is even more magnificent: in the 1820s the Town Council had had some difficulty in keeping under control builders who overstepped planning requirements in the interests of economy or to satisfy a client's whim, but when the Earl of Moray decided to develop 'the lands of Drumsheugh', he took care, as a landowner, to ensure an overall restraint in the plan by Gillespie Graham. The flowing lines of Randolph Crescent, Ainslie Place and Moray Place, all threaded on Great Stuart Street, are the result –

Robert Adam's church design, instead using a cheaper plan from Robert Reid. This turned out as St George's Church, with its copper dome – one of the Edinburgh skyline's most distinguished elements. Many experts, almost from the date of its completion, have, however, expressed dissatisfaction with the overall effect of what is now West Register House, no matter how pleasing its dome. In Professor Youngson's timeless book on the architecture of the capital *The Making of Classical Edinburgh*, he goes as far as to suggest that 'the New Town has suffered a twin misfortune in its churches, for St Andrew's is the right church in the wrong place, and St George's is the wrong church in the right place' – which also proves that architectural tastelessness is not exclusively the province of the twentieth-century planner.

Left: The restored kitchen in the Georgian House, 7 Charlotte Square, Edinburgh. Reproduced by courtesy of the National Trust for Scotland. *Below:* The parlour or back drawing-room in the Georgian House. Reproduced by courtesy of the National Trust for Scotland

A gauche: La cuisine restaurée de la « Georgian House », 7 Charlotte Square, Edimbourg. *Ci-dessous:* Le parloir, ou salon de derrière, de la « Georgian House »

Links: Die restaurierte Küche in dem georgianischen Haus Nr. 7, in Charlotte Square, Edinburgh. *Unten:* Salon oder hinteres Wohnzimmer im georgianischen Haus

Top: West Register House (formerly St George's Church). *Above:* St George's Church and the west side of Charlotte Square. *Above right:* Part of Royal Circus. *Right:* North-west angle of Moray Place

Coin supérieur: « West Register House » (précédemment église St-George). *Ci-dessus:* L'église St-George et le côté gauche de « Charlotte Square ». *Ci-dessus à droite:* Une partie du « Royal Circus ». *A droite:* Angle nord-ouest de « Moray Place »

Oben: Das West Register Hause (früher St. Georgskirche). *Oben:* St. Georgskirche an der westlichen Seite vom Charlotte Square. *Oben rechts:* Teil des königlichen Zirkus. *Rechts:* Nordwestliche Sicht des Moray Platz

and they survive complete with 'pleasure gardens'.

Obviously, the neo-classicism did not express itself exclusively in domestic architecture, as Register House had already proved. Edinburgh's distinctive skyline owes much to the array of extraordinary buildings on Calton Hill. The first of these, the Old Observatory, dates from 1776 and is of interest as the only example within the city of the work of James Craig (he of the first city plan, which did not require him to supply designs for individual buildings). Nearby is the 'New' Observatory, by the prolific Playfair, who also had a hand in the Dugald Stewart Memorial, loosely modelled on the monument of Lysicrates in Athens – and closely resembling the Burns Memorial lower down the hill. Back on the windy summit, the Nelson Monument by William Burn looms over the steep, tree-clad slope that leads down to Regent Road, but most spectacular is the National Monument, designed, once again, by Playfair. Invoking a strange mixture of grandeur and pathos it started life with the intention of becoming an exact model of the Parthenon. In 1822, the foundation stone of this architectural white elephant was laid, but by 1829, funds had run out – and it remains unfinished to this day.

Doubtless, as the stone of the National Memorial was laid with due ceremony, the civic dignitaries in the gathering would have paused to look back towards the newly completed development around Waterloo Bridge. Across a deep gully, now the lair of aggressive, scurrying Post Office vans, had been thrown a fine bridge, complete with Corinthian triumphal arches. Significantly, a deliberate decision had been taken to construct the bridge so as to let pedestrians appreciate the views from it. Easily overlooked by

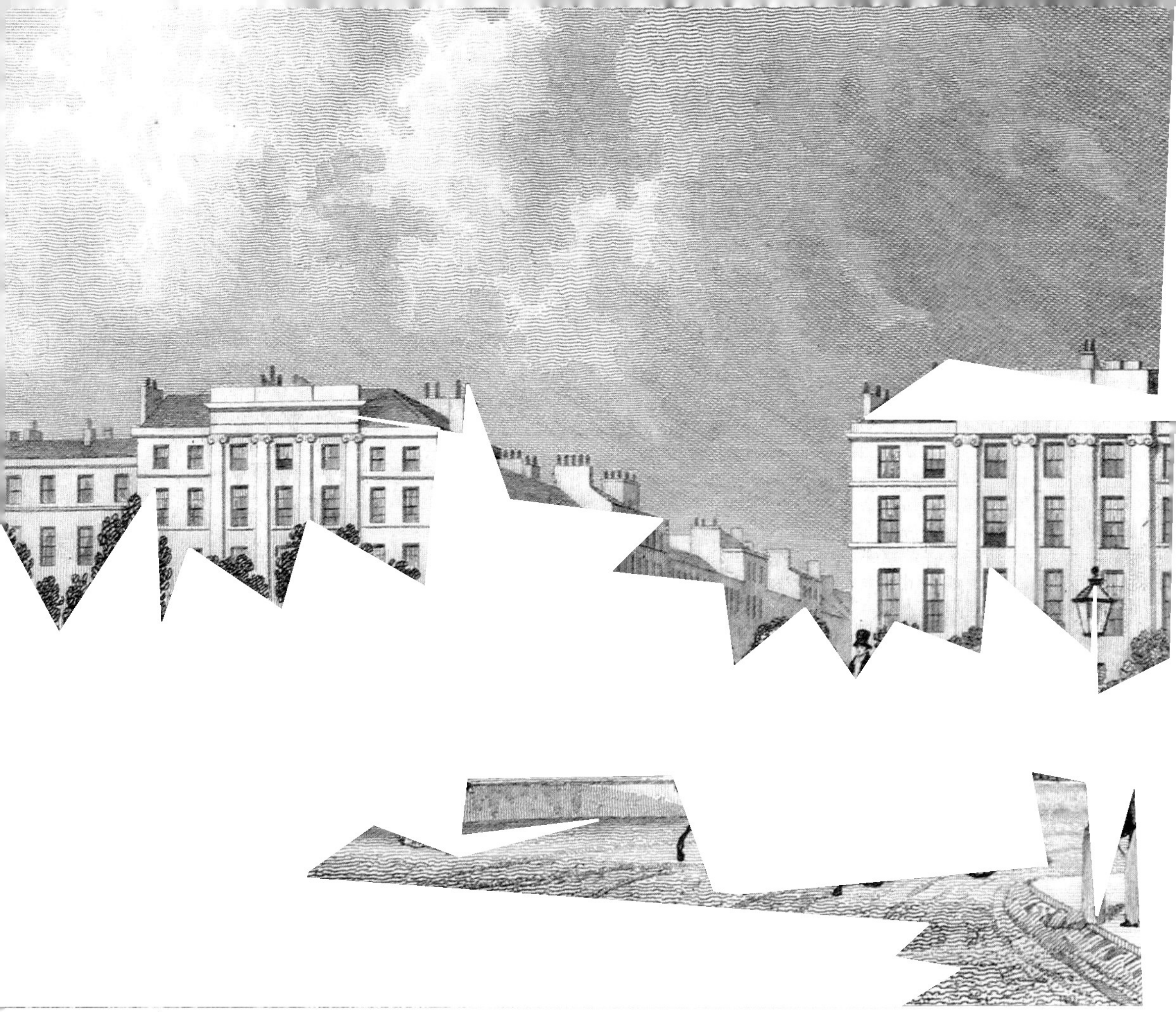

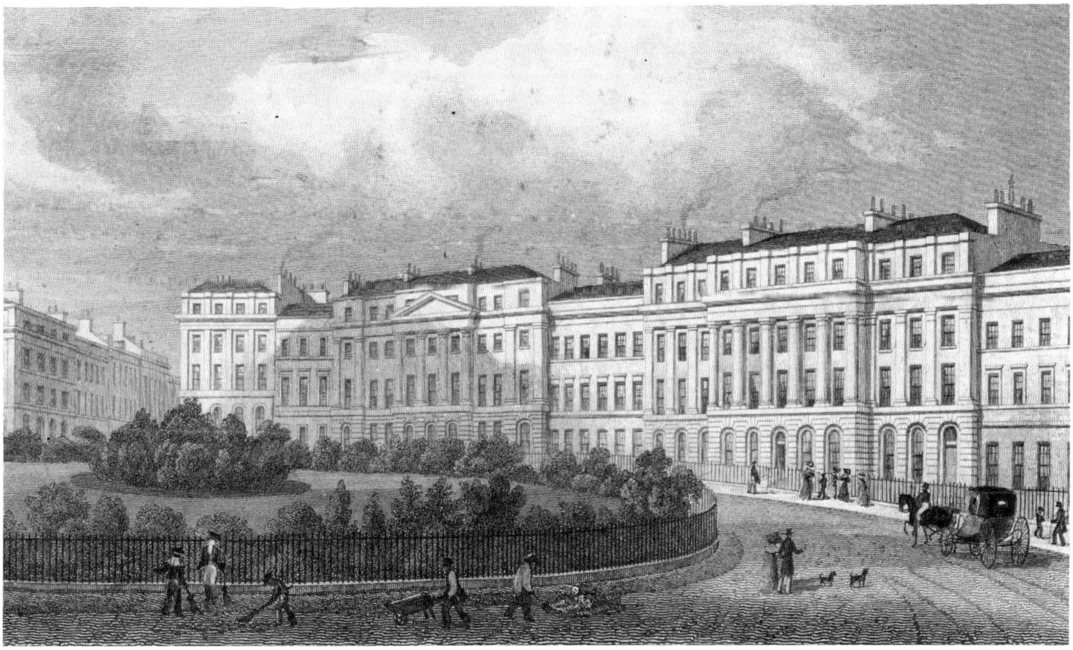

visitors approaching from the east, in the pause before plunging on to Princes Street, the bridge's Corinthian 'triumphal' arches are themselves a triumph – of successful planning. The designer, Archibald Elliott, even included a screen wall along the base of Calton Hill, which extends the vista from Princes Street past the severe symmetry of the buildings flanking Waterloo Place and on to the complex skyline of the hill itself.

The Edinburgh of today was happening, it seemed, all in a rush in the 1820s. Some of the finest architects of the day were involved in a dragged-out dispute on exactly the best route for the Mound – which was by this time accumulating, with the Council's blessing, hundreds of tons of earth excavated from other parts of the New Town's foundations. By the 1830s, it had assumed its present course on a proper roadway. At its northern end, Playfair (again) had completed the first version of what is now the Royal Scottish Academy by 1826. This seems to have pleased nobody, but his reworking and extension, though expensive, met with great approval on completion in 1835. His National Gallery of Scotland, just behind, was completed in the year of his death, 1857. Visitors can note the severity of the Doric columns, though fluted, on the first building and compare them to the gentler Ionic style of the later work.

In the thirty years between these two public buildings that lend so much distinction to the mound, linking Old Town with New, another famous landmark was added to the skyline – the Scott Monument. Completed in 1844, no classical restraint was exhibited by its architect, George Kemp. Instead, he conceived a fantasy in Gothic, with details copied from Scott's much-loved Melrose Abbey – pillars, niches and pinnacles in profusion, bedecked with statuettes from Scott's novels, with the master himself in marble staring solemnly out at the hurrying Princes Street crowds.

The 1820s also saw the completion of the University buildings – the Old College. These had been started in the time of Robert Adam, in 1789, when he would also have been involved in his Charlotte Square contract. Shortage of cash and the Napoleonic Wars, however, hampered the development, and Adam himself died in 1792. Playfair was the architect responsible for much modification to the original design. Of particular note in this grand range of buildings are the monolithic columns, specified by Adam, which support the portico. Perhaps, in a sense, 'new' architecture met 'old' town – the south side of the Old College was built on the line of the old Flodden Wall, running parallel to Chambers Street.

Opposite above: Ainslie Place. *Opposite below:* The Dugald Stewart Memorial. *Left:* The Nelson Monument on Calton Hill. *Below:* The National Monument

Ci-contre en haut: « Ainslie Place ». *Ci-contre en bas:* « Dugald Stewart Memorial ». *A gauche:* « Nelson Monument » sur « Calton Hill ». *Ci-dessous:* Le « National Monument »

Gegenüber, oben: Ainslie Platz. *Gegenüber, unten:* Die Dugald Stewart Gedenkstätte. *Links:* Das Nelsondenkmal auf dem Calton Hügel. *Unten:* Das Nationaldenkmal

Les plans de Robert Adam pour l'église St Georges dans Charlotte Square furent abandonnés au profit de ceux de Robert Reid, considérés plus économiques. Malgré un dôme imposant, ce bâtiment (maintenant West Register House) ne fit jamais l'unanimité.

La deuxième phase de la « ville nouvelle », de lignes moins sévères, se poursuivit avec la construction à partir de 1820, des quartiers situés sur les pentes descendant vers la vallée de la Water of Leith, avec notamment les magnifiques Royal Circus, Moray Place, Randolph Crescent et Ainslie Place.

Le style néo-classique n'affecta pas exclusivement les habitations résidentielles, ainsi qu'en témoignent les imposantes constructions à caractère public situées sur Calton Hill: Old Observatory (1776), le « New » Observatory, le Dugald Stewart Memorial (sur un modèle grec) et le Burns Memorial plus bas. Le Nelson Monument et le National Monument occupent tous les deux un emplacement des plus spectaculaires. Ce dernier, destiné à être une reproduction exacte du Parthénon, ne fut jamais terminé.

C'est également dans les années 1820 que se développa Waterloo Bridge, construit, dans le style Corinthien, en vue de permettre aux piétons d'apprécier les panoramas spectaculaires qu'il offre sur la ville.

Le Mound, rue construite sur un promontoire fait des tonnes de terre provenant des excavations de la ville, fut réalisé en 1830 et suivi de la Royal Scottish Academy (1835) et de la National Gallery of Scotland (1857). Le Monument à

Walter Scott (terminé en 1844) est, lui, loin de la sobriété georgienne, avec ses colonnes, niches et pinacles « gothiques » typiques de l'ère victorienne.

C'est également vers les années 1820 que furent terminés les batiments de l'université.

Die zweite Bauphase der Neustadt begann um 1820. Die geschwungene Häuserreihe von Royal Circus, Moray Place und Randolph Crescent, Ainslie Place und Moray Place, die alle in Great Stuart Street mündeten, waren das Ergebnis.

Großartige, öffentliche Gebäude im klassizistischen Stil sind die Häuser auf Calton Hill, die alte Sternwarte von James Craig entworfen, nahebei die neue Sternwarte von Playfair, der auch das Dugald Stewart Denkmal entwarf, welches dem Denkmal des Lysikrates in Athen nachempfunden ist und dem Burns Denkmal ähnelt. Weiter den Hügel herauf steht William Burn's imposantes Nelson Denkmal. Beeindruckend ist auch das Nationalmonument von Playfair, 1822 begonnen, aber wegen Geldmangel nie vollendet. Von Archibald Elliott stammt die großartige Brücke mit ihren korinthischen Triumphbögen.

Im Jahre 1826 wurde die königliche schottische Akademie — ebenfalls von Playfair — begonnen und 1835 vollendet. Die Nationalgalerie von Schottland liegt direkt dahinter und würde in seinem Todesjahr 1857 vollendet. Das Scott-Monument ist ein weiterer berühmter Markstein für Edinburgh und den berühmten Dichter. In den 1820er Jahren wurden auch die Universitätsgebäude — das alte Kolleg — beendet.

Modernity pressed on. A proposal to build a railway through Princes Street Gardens was opposed by the Princes Street Proprietors in 1836 – but by 1845 commercial interests had overruled the objectors. Over the next twenty years, all around, series of contemporary landmarks were appearing – the Theatre Royal was demolished to make way for the General Post Office in Waterloo Place, completed in 1866, while the imposing Bank of Scotland on the Mound assumed its present form by 1868. If commercial life was blossoming, then education was served by the Royal Scottish Museum, also opened in 1866. Curiously, only a few years later, houses built in the first wave of the city's eighteenth-century expansion were demolished to build the present-day Chambers Street, on which the museum stands. This echoes the much later demolition, in 1971, of most of St James's Square for the construction of the controversial St James's Centre, the city's shopping mall that intrudes its bulk on the skyline, particularly noticeable from the Botanic Gardens.

Opposite above: The Royal High School below Calton Hill. *Opposite below:* The National Gallery of Scotland. *Below left:* Lady Stair's House, the Royal Mile, Edinburgh. *Below:* The Old College, University of Edinburgh

Ci-contre en haut: La « Royal High School » en contrebas de « Calton Hill ». *Ci-contre en bas:* La « National Gallery of Scotland ». *Ci-dessous à gauche:* La maison de Lady Stair, « Royal Mile », Edimbourg. *Ci-dessous:* « Old College », Université d'Edimbourg

Gegenüber, oben: Das königliche Gymnasium unterhalb des Calton Hügel. *Gegenüber, unten:* Die Nationalgallerie Schottlands. *Unten links:* Lady Stairs Haus, Die Königliche Meile, Edinburgh. *Unten:* Das alte Kolleg, Edinburgh Universität

However, much of Edinburgh's neo-classical architecture has survived into the twentieth century (and, of course, so have considerable chunks of the Old Town, successfully renovated in the Canongate and Lawnmarket, as well as some Grassmarket restoration). The city's longest neo-classical façade is that of Royal Terrace, which overlooks an area of the city which was never completed to the grand scheme conceived by Playfair. For the very best of the surviving architecture, the visitor must look further to the west of the city.

Modern Edinburgh lives and works with its history part of its everyday life – the one o'clock gun booms out every day, the old Palace of Holyrood plays host to royal visitors, even some of the drawing rooms of the New Town still witness elegant parties, though the sedan chairs may have been replaced by gleaming horseless carriages. The visitor to Edinburgh will be struck by this sense of continuity. The historic city is also the everyday city, and Scotland's capital continues to play an important role in the commercial and artistic life of the nation.

Avec l'arrivée du chemin de fer, construit malgré l'opposition des résidents, en 1845, Edimbourg entra véritablement dans les temps modernes. A noter, en particulier, le General Post Office dans Waterloo Place (1866), la Bank of Scotland sur le Mound (1868) et le Royal Scottish Museum (1866). Plus près de nous, la démolition de la plus grande partie de St James's Square pour faire place au centre commercial du même nom, fut des plus controversées.

Une grande partie de l'architecture georgienne d'Edimbourg a cependant survécu jusqu'à nos jours (ainsi que des parties plus anciennes de la ville). L'Edimbourg de la fin du 20ᵉ siècle vit avec son histoire mais la cité historique est aussi la ville de tous les jours, et la capitale de l'Ecosse continue à jouer un rôle important dans la vie commerciale et artistique de la nation.

An modernen Gebäuden und Projekten folgten eine Eisenbahnlinie durch die Princes Street Gärten, Das Hauptpostamt in Waterloo Place (1866), die imposante Bank von Schottland (1868) und das königlich-

Above left: Waverley Bridge in the late nineteenth century. *Above right:* The Assembly Hall and Ramsay Gardens

Ci-dessus à gauche: « Waverley Bridge » vers la fin du dix-neuvième siècle. *Ci-dessus à droite:* « Assembly Hall » et « Ramsay Gardens »

Oben links: Waverley Brücke im späten 19. Jhs. *Oben rechts:* Festsaal und Ramsay Gärten

schottische Museum (1866).

Viele von Edinburghs klassizistischen Gebäuden haben überlebt, viele Teile der alten Stadt in Canongate und Lawnmarket und Grassmarket sind erfolgreich restauriert worden.

Das tägliche Leben im modernen Edinburgh ist verwoben mit seiner Vergangenheit und die ehrwürdigen alten Gebäude spielen beim Besuch von königlichen Gästen, beim Representieren und Festlichkeiten eine große Rolle. Schottlands Hauptstadt nimmt nach wie vor einen wichtigen Teil im kommerziellen und künstlerischen Leben der Nation ein.

Around Edinburgh

Confined within its walls, Scotland's capital only expanded to swallow nearby villages from the eighteenth century onwards. Corstorphine, now a busy suburb west of the city, was once separated from it by a marsh. Travellers guided themselves across it by a lamp kept constantly burning in Corstorphine Kirk. Dean Village, an ancient milling community on the Water of Leith, once clustered round the old road northwards out of the city, till it was bypassed by Telford's Dean Bridge in 1832. Lying much further to the west is Colinton, another settlement originally dependent on the Water of Leith to power its mill wheels. Now it provides leafy walkways along the banks of the river.

Separated from the city by the great upthrust of Arthur's Seat, Duddingston Village still has a watch-tower in its kirkyard, to guard against bodysnatchers. (Their unsavoury method of supplying medical researchers has resulted in a number of these towers around the city, notably at the New Calton Burial Ground and on King's Stables Road, only a moment from Princes Street.) Other relics of former time still to be seen near Duddingston Kirk include the 'jougs' – an iron collar attached to the church wall. It used to be attached also to the neck of a wrongdoer, in view of the congregation!

Of the seaward parts of the city, Leith is the most ancient. Now experiencing a revival, with renovated properties and fashionable restaurants replacing some of the older warehouses, the port of Leith was trading even before Robert the Bruce mentions it in his Charter to Edinburgh in 1329. Of its many distinctions must be included its claim (hotly disputed by St Andrew's) that Leith is the true home of golf. A course was laid out on its links as early as 1593.

Further east the exotically named Portobello owes its development to a sailor familiar with Puerto Bello in Panama, captured in 1739. He built a house in the gorsy, spray-washed open land within sight of Arthur's Seat. A bed of clay subsequently gave rise to a pottery industry within the community, but its main growth came with the vogue for sea-bathing, already under way by the end of the eighteenth century. Holiday homes were built, from simple Georgian to indulgent Victorian villas, as discreet retreats from the city. Today, Portobello still offers the visitor the flavour of a seaside resort wth bracing walks along the promenade and a sandy beach.

Cramond marks the western extremity of the city's coastline. The Romans knew it as Alaterva, and from time to time further evidence of their settlement is uncovered. But like Dean Village and Colinton further upstream, the community owes its origin to the river's water-power. Present-day strollers by the yachts at anchor will find it hard to imagine that before the end of the eighteenth century, the industrial revolution had arrived in the form of an ironworks, while paper and furniture-making in former times also disturbed the peace of this pleasant village.

Ce n'est qu'à partir du dix-huitième siècle que la capitale de l'Ecosse, jusqu'alors confinée entre ses murs, s'étendit pour englober les villages alentour. Corstorphine, à l'ouest, est aujourd'hui une banlieue animée. Dean Village, au nord, et Colinton, plus à l'ouest, étaient tous deux des communautés minotières anciennes sur la rivière « Water of Leith ».

Au delà de « Arthur's Seat », Duddington Village possède toujours dans son cimetière une tour de garde contre les déterreurs de cadavres pour la recherche médicale. Autre vestige des environs: le « joug », collier d'acier scellé dans le mur des églises pour exposer les malfaiteurs aux fidèles.

Côté mer, Leith, dont les activités portuaires remontent à avant 1329, date à laquelle il est cité par Robert The Bruce, est aujourd'hui en pleine renaissance et restauration. Leith se veut également le berceau du golf, privilège contesté par St Andrew's.

Plus à l'est, Portobello doit son développement à un marin qui connaissait bien Puerto Bello au Panama, puis à l'industrie de la poterie, et enfin et surtout, dès avant la fin du dix-huitième siècle, à la vogue pour les bains de mer. Aujourd'hui, l'atmosphère de station balnéaire y est toujours présente.

Cramond (Alaterva pour les Romains) marque à l'ouest les confins de la ville sur la côte. Malgré la présence romaine, c'est à l'énergie de la rivière que, comme Dean Village et Colinton, Cramond doit son essor. Difficile aujourd'hui d'imaginer, en voyant les yachts à l'ancre, les usines sidérurgiques de la révolution industrielle.

Die von Stadtmauern begrenzte Hauptstadt Schottlands vergrößerte sich vom 18. Jh. an durch Eingemeindung der umliegenden Dörfer. Corstorphine, heute belebter Vorort westlich der Stadt, war einst durch einen Sumpf von ihr getrennt. Dean Village war eine alte Mühlensiedlung am Leith. Weiter westlich liegt Colington, dessen Mühlenräder ebenfalls vom Wasser des Leith angetrieben wurden. Heute sind hier schöne Flußpromenaden. Das Dorf Duddington hat in seinem Kirchhof noch immer einen Wachtturm erbaut gegen Leichenräuber.

Leith ist der älteste Stadtteil an der See. Es erlebt zur Zeit einen Aufschwung. Alte Anwesen werden renoviert, Lagerhäuser nachen modernen Restaurants Platz. Leith rühmt sich auch die Wiege des Golfs zu sein, ein Anspruch, der St. Andrews auf das schärfste bestreitet. Weiter östlich liegt der Stadtteil Portobelle, der seinen exotischen Namen von Puerto Bello in Panama ableitet. Die Entdeckung eines Lehmbettes führte zur Töpfereiindustrie, doch Haupteinnahme wurde die im 18. Jh. beginnende Idee des Seebadens, die zum Bau von schönen Villen führte. Portobelle hat prächtige Seepromenaden und sandigen Strand. Cramond markiert den westlichsten Küstenstreifen der Stadt. Die Römer nannten ihn Alaterva. Doch wie Dean Village und Colington verdankt auch Cramond seine Gründung dem Fluß. Urlauber, die hier ihre Boote ankern, können sich kaum vorstellen, daß der Frieden dieses entzückenden Dorfes einst durch Eisenwerke und Papier- und Möbelindustrie gestört wurde.

Above: Dean Village
Opposite: Regent Terrace

Ci-dessus: « Dean Village »
Ci-contre: « Regent Terrace »

Oben: Dorf Dean
Gegenüber: Regent Terrasse

ISBN 0–7117–0218–7
© 1986 Jarrold Colour Publications
Printed and published in Great Britain by Jarrold and Sons Ltd, Norwich. 186